T5-DHH-212

Presented to

_____

On this _____ day of _____

By _____

With this special message:

_____

_____

_____

itty**bitty**books™

A Time For Love

THOMAS NELSON PUBLISHERS
Nashville, Tennessee

Copyright © 1994 by Thomas Nelson
Publishers.

Published in Nashville, Tennessee by
Thomas Nelson Publishers.

**Library of Congress
Cataloging-in-Publication Data**

A Time for love.
    p. cm. — (Itty Bitty books)
    ISBN 0-8407-6337-9 (TR)
    ISBN 0-7852-8338-2 (MM)
    1. Love—Quotations, maxims, etc.
2. Love—Poetry.   I. Series: Itty Bitty
book.
PN6084.L6T56   1994
808.88′2—dc20   93-24368
                                         CIP

Printed in Singapore.
1 2 3 4 5 — 98 97 96 95 94

INTRODUCTION

There are probably more songs sung and more books written about love than about any other single subject. After all, it's love that makes the world go 'round. The words within this little volume are some of the best ever written or spoken on the subject and they are dedicated to you—with love. I hope that we will always make A TIME FOR LOVE in our lives.

To everything there is a
season,
A time for every purpose
under heaven . . .
A time to love, . . .

Ecclesiastes 3:1, 8
(NKJV)

As for me, to love you alone, to make you happy, to do nothing which would contradict your wishes, this is my destiny and the aim of my life.

Napoleon Bonaparte to Josephine, 1796

Love makes all hard hearts
gentle.

―――

George Herbert

Love has always been the motivating force in my life.

Kathleen Fraser

Love is the thing that
enables a woman to sing
while she mops up the floor
after her husband has walked
across it in his barn boots.

Anonymous

While faith makes all things possible, it is love that makes all things easy.

Evan Hopkins

Love is the extremely difficult realization that something other than oneself is real.

Iris Murdoch

The love of wealth makes
bitter men; the love of God,
better men.

W. L. Hudson

If we are to make a mature adjustment to life, we must be able to give and receive love.

Anna Trego Hunter

The Eskimos had fifty-two names for snow because it was important to them; there ought to be as many for love.

Margaret Atwood

It is a beautiful necessity of
our nature to love something.

Douglas Jerrold

The highest happiness on earth is in marriage. Every man who is happily married is a successful man even if he has failed in everything else.

William Lyon Phelps

Little deeds of kindness,
Little words of love,
Make our world an Eden
Like the heaven above.

Julia A. Fletcher
Carney

In a great romance, each person plays a part that the other really likes.

Elizabeth Ashley

If we spend our lives in loving, we have no leisure to complain, or to feel unhappiness.

Joseph Joubert

By the accident of fortune a man may rule the world for a time, but by virtue of love he may rule the world forever.

Lao-tze

Man, while he loves, is never quite depraved.

Charles Lamb

If only one could tell true love from false love as one can tell mushrooms from toadstools.

Katherine Mansfield

If all the world and love were
   young,
And truth in every shepherd's
   tongue,
These pretty pleasures might
   me move
To live with thee, and be thy
   love.

———

Sir Walter Raleigh

When a man is in love
with one woman in a family,
it is astonishing how fond he
becomes of every person
connected with it.

William M. Thackeray

The love that kept us
through the passing night
will guide and keep us still.

Anonymous

Love is a deep well from which you may drink often, but into which you may fall but once.

Ellye Howell Glover

Love does not begin and
end the way we seem to think
it does. Love is battle, love is
a war; love is a growing up.

James Baldwin

A good marriage is the union of two forgivers.

Ruth Bell Graham

Love endures only when the lovers love many things together and not merely each other.

Walter Lippman

T wo human loves make one
divine.

Elizabeth Barrett
Browning

It is the child in us who loves.

Anne Morrow
Lindbergh

It is with true love as with ghosts. Everyone talks of it, but few have ever seen it.

Francois, Duc de La Rochefoucauld

Love rules his kingdom
without a sword.

George Herbert

There's no vocabulary
For love within a family, love
        that's lived in
But not looked at, love within
        the light of which
All else is seen, the love
        within which
All other love finds speech.
This love is silent.

———

T. S. Eliot

It is not the most lovable individuals who stand more in need of love, but the most unlovable.

———

Ashley Montagu

Above all things have fervent love for one another, for "love will cover a multitude of sins."

1 Peter 4:8 (NKJV)

As you get older, I think
you need to put your arms
around each other more.

Barbara Bush

Love that stammers, that stutters, is apt to be the love that loves best.

———

Gabriela Mistral

A happy marriage is a long conversation that always seems too short.

André Maurois

He brought me to the banqueting house,
And his banner over me was love.

Song of Solomon 2:4
(NKJV)

N o fame, were the best less
 brittle,
No praise, were it wide as
 earth,
Is worth so much as a little
 Child's love may be worth.

Algernon Charles
Swinburne

Make sure you never, never argue at night. You just lose a good night's sleep, and you can't settle anything until morning anyway.

Rose Kennedy

All love should be simply stepping-stones to the love of God. So it was with me; and blessed be his name for his great goodness and mercy.

Plato

Look 'round our world;
    behold the chain of love
Combining all below and all
    above.

Alexander Pope

Love is a little blind; when we love someone dearly we unconsciously overlook many faults.

Beatrice Saunders

No matter what the subject, the subject is always love.

Ingrid Bengis

Marriage is our last, best chance to grow up.

———

Joseph Barth

The heart can do anything.

———

Molière

I have a heart with room for every joy.

Philip James Bailey

Love is to the moral nature
exactly what the sun is to the
earth.

Honoré de Balzac

Love is like an hourglass, with the heart filling up as the brain empties.

Jules Renard

Love is not a possession but a growth. The heart is a lamp with just oil enough to burn for an hour, and if there be no oil to put in again its light will go out. God's grace is the oil that fills the lamp of love.

———

Henry Ward Beecher

A happy marriage has in it
all the pleasures of friendship,
all the enjoyments of sense
and reason, and, indeed, all
the sweets of life.

Joseph Addison

Love demands all, and has a right to all.

———

Ludwig von Beethoven

Until I truly loved, I was alone.

Caroline Norton

Love is the May-day of the heart.

Benjamin Disraeli

Love and a cough cannot be hid.

George Herbert

There is no instinct like
that of the heart.

———————

Lord Byron

Let me not to the marriage
of true minds
Admit impediments: love is
not love
Which alters when it
alteration finds.

William Shakespeare

No man knows what the wife of his bosom is until he has gone with her through the fiery trials of this world.

Washington Irving

They gave each other a smile with a future in it.

———

Ring Lardner

A "bit of love" is the only bit that will bridle the tongue.

Fred Beck

Love cannot be coaxed and teased. It comes out of Heaven, unasked and unsought.

———

Pearl S. Buck

The rose is sweetest wash'd
with morning dew,
And Love is loveliest when
embalm'd in tears.

Sir Walter Scott

Love can hope where reason
would despair.

George, Baron
Lyttelton

Love is love's reward.

John Dryden

Speak low if you speak love.

William Shakespeare

One word frees us of all the weight and pain of life; that word is love.

Sophocles

Grow old along with me!
The best is yet to be.

Robert Browning

Man can live his truth, his deepest truth, but he cannot speak it. It is for this reason that love becomes the ultimate human answer to the ultimate human question.

———

Archibald MacLeish

Talk not of wasted affection; affection never was wasted.

———————

Henry Wadsworth
Longfellow

It is as healthy to enjoy
sentiment as to enjoy jam.

G. K. Chesterton

Love sought is good, but given unsought is better.

William Shakespeare

An ideal husband is one who treats his wife like a new car.

———————

Dan Bennett

W isdom has nothing to do with love.

Philip Barry

If you want to know how your girl will treat you after marriage, just listen to her talking to her little brother.

Sam Levenson

If love were what the rose is,
And I were like the leaf,
Our lives would grow together
In sad or singing weather.

Algernon Charles
Swinburne

In our life there is a single color, as on an artist's palette, which provides the meaning of life and art. It is the color of love.

Marc Chagall

Life is to be fortified by many friendships. To love and be loved is the greatest happiness of existence.

———

Sydney Smith

Fidelity is knowing who you belong to and having the decency to pass up the rest.

Ann Landers

Love is never lost. If not reciprocated it will flow back and soften and purify the heart.

Washington Irving

There is no love which does not become help.

Paul Tillich

Love looks through a telescope; envy, through a microscope.

Josh Billings

Not where I breathe, but where I love, I live.

Robert Southwell

There is no remedy for love
but to love more.

Henry David Thoreau

Always I have a chair for you in the smallest parlor in the world, to wit, my heart.

Emily Dickinson

The invisible path of
gravity liberates the stone.
The invisible slope of love
liberates man.

Antoine de
Saint-Exupery

Joy is love's consciousness.
Peace is love's confidence.
Patience is love's habit.
Kindness is love's vitality.
Goodness is love's activity.
Faithfulness is love's quantity.
Meekness is love's tone.
Temperance is love's victory.

G. Campbell Morgan

To the one
I love

It is only with the heart that one can see rightly; what is essential is invisible to the eye.

———

Antoine de
Saint-Exupery

Mind is the partial side of man; the heart is everything.

Antoine de Rivarol

Whoever loves true life
will love true love.

———

Elizabeth Barrett
Browning

I love you more than
yesterday, less than tomorrow.

Edmond Rostand

There is no greater love
than the love that holds on
where there seems nothing
left to hold on to.

G. W. C. Thomas

Love is a tender plant; when properly nourished, it becomes sturdy and enduring, but neglected it will soon wither and die.

———

Hugh B. Brown

One of the great illusions of our time is that love is self-sustaining. It is not. Love must be fed and nurtured, constantly renewed. That demands ingenuity and consideration, but first and foremost it demands time.

David R. Mace

Loving a child doesn't mean giving in to all his whims; to love him is to bring out the best in him, to teach him to love what is difficult.

Nadia Boulanger

Love does not die easily. It is a living thing. It thrives in the face of all life's hazards, save one—neglect.

James D. Bryden

Lukewarmness I account a
  sin,
As great in love as in religion.

Abraham Cowley

Love is the master key that opens the gates of happiness.

Oliver Wendell Holmes

There is no surprise more magical than the surprise of being loved: it is God's finger on man's shoulder.

Charles Morgan

Of all the earthly music that reaches farthest into heaven is the beating of a truly loving heart.

———

Henry Ward Beecher

Be of love (a little) more careful than of anything.

e. e. cummings

There is nothing so loyal as love.

Alice Cary

We are all born for love; it is the principle of existence and its only end.

Benjamin Disraeli

Love, indeed, lends a precious seeing to the eye, and hearing to the ear: all sights and sounds are glorified by the light of its presence.

Frederick Saunders

How do I love thee? Let me count the ways.
I love thee to the depth and breadth and height
My soul can reach, when feeling out of sight
For the ends of Being and ideal Grace.

Elizabeth Barrett
Browning

Take this, with warmest love,
Tho Fans are, as a rule,
Considered efficacious
In keaping people cool.

Love is a symbol of eternity.
It wipes out all sense of time,
destroying all memory of a
beginning and all fear of an
end.

―――――――

Madame de Stael

It is astonishing how little
one feels poverty when one
loves.

———————

John Bulwer

My wife is, in the strictest sense, my sole companion, and I need no other. There is no vacancy in my mind any more than in my heart.

Nathaniel Hawthorne

At the touch of love
everyone becomes a poet.

Plato

I should like to call you
by all the endearing
epithets, and yet I can
find no lovelier word than
the simple word "dear."

———

Robert Schumann

Love is ever the beginning of knowledge, as fire is of light.

Thomas Carlyle

Eve was not taken out of Adam's head to top him, neither out of his feet to be trampled on by him, but out of his side to be equal with him, under his arm to be protected by him, and near his heart to be loved by him.

Matthew Henry

Thou art my life, my love,
  my heart,
   The very eyes of me:
And hast command of every
      part
To live and die for thee.

———

Robert Herrick

A good marriage is that in which each appoints the other the guardian of his solitude.

Rainer Maria Rilke

All, everything that I understand, I understand only because I love.

Leo Tolstoy

I like not only to be loved,
but to be told that I am loved;
the realm of silence is large
enough beyond the grave.

George Eliot

A successful marriage requires falling in love many times, always with the same person.

Mignon McLaughlin

Love blinds all men alike,
both the reasonable and the
foolish.

Menander

Such ever was love's way; to rise, it stoops.

Robert Browning

To love and be loved is to feel the sun from both sides.

David Viscott

There is nothing holier, in this life of ours, than the first consciousness of love—the first fluttering of its silken wings.

Henry Wadsworth
Longfellow

It is love that asks, that seeks, that knocks, that finds, and that is faithful to what it finds.

St. Augustine

Come live with me and be
    my love,
And we will all the pleasures
    prove
That valleys, groves, hills, and
    fields,
Woods or steepy mountain
    yields.

Christopher Marlowe

Love—what you keep to yourself you lose, what you give away you keep forever.

***

Anonymous

Hatred stirs up strife,
But love covers all sins.

Proverbs 10:12 (NKJV)

There are three principal postures of love. It gives with joy, receives with appreciation and rebukes with humility and hope.

Albert M. Wells, Jr.

When we love, we give up
the center of ourselves.

———

Rollo May

Take love when love is
given,
But never think to find it
A sure escape from sorrow
Or a complete repose.

Sara Teasdale

All love is sweet,
Given or returned.
Common as light is love,
And its familiar voice
wearies not ever.

Percy Bysshe Shelley

How often has it been said that a marriage is not truly a marriage unless it is first a friendship? How true this is, and how true that the satisfaction found in friendship lies not so much in achieving interpersonal skills as in developing ways and times of relating that build meaning upon meaning.

Lesley Barfoot

There are six requisites in every happy marriage. The first is Faith and the remaining five are Confidence.

Elbert Hubbard

There is no happiness comparable to that of the first hand-clasp, when the one asks: "Do you love me?" and the other replies, "Yes."

Guy de Maupassant

A heart as soft,
A heart as kind,
A heart as sound and free
  As in the whole world thou
    cans't find,
That heart I'll give to thee.

———

Robert Herrick

Familiar acts are beautiful
through love.

Percy Bysshe Shelley

To love deeply in one direction makes us more loving in all others.

Madame Swetchnie

It is ever the invisible that is the object of our profoundest worship. With the lover it is not the seen but the unseen that he muses upon.

Christian Nestell
Bovee

A man is only as good as
what he loves.

Saul Bellow

Marriages are made in heaven.

John Lyly

A single man . . . is an incomplete animal. He resembles the odd half of a pair of scissors.

Benjamin Franklin

W hen love and skill work together expect a masterpiece.

John Ruskin

In lovers' quarrels, the party that loves most is always most willing to acknowledge the greater fault.

Sir Walter Scott

Trouble is a part of your life, and if you don't share it, you don't give the person who loves you enough chance to love you enough.

Dinah Shore

The love we have in our youth is superficial compared to the love that an old man has for his old wife.

Will Durant

So long as we love, we
serve. So long as we are loved
by others, I would almost say
we are indispensable; and no
man is useless while he has a
friend.

Robert Louis
Stevenson

Delicacy is to love what grace is to beauty.

Madame de Maintenon

Where love is, there is God also.

Leo Tolstoy

Love is like a beautiful
flower which I may not touch,
but whose fragrance makes
the garden a place of delight
just the same.

Helen Keller

In marriage do thou be wise:
Prefer the person before
money, virtue before beauty,
the mind before the body,
then thou hast a wife, a
friend, a companion, a second
self.

———

William Penn

Chains do not hold a marriage together. It is threads, hundreds of tiny threads, which sew people together through the years.

Simone Signoret

Absence sharpens love;
presence strengthens it.

Thomas Fuller

Love God completely; love others compassionately; love yourself correctly.

Anonymous

Love is the forgetting of oneself in the service of another.

R. Ainsley Barnwell

One good husband is worth two good wives, for the scarcer things are the more they're valued.

Benjamin Franklin

Love can stand anything but distance.

Allen Dace

Love is the life of man.

Emanuel Swedenborg

Love is a spirit all compact
of fire.

William Shakespeare

Love, which is the essence of God, is not for levity, but for the total worth of man.

Ralph Waldo Emerson

Lust and desire cannot wait.
True love can.

Walter A. Kortrey

Marriage is not just spiritual communion and passionate embraces; marriage is also three meals a day, sharing the workload, and remembering to carry out the trash.

Dr. Joyce Brothers

Love reckons hours for months, and days for years; and every little absence is an age.

John Dryden

For love's humility is love's true pride.

———————

Bayard Taylor

No sky is heavy if the heart
be light.

———

Charles Churchill

We don't believe in
rheumatism and true love
until after the first attack.

Marie von
Ebner-Eschenbach

As selfishness and complaint pervert and cloud the mind, so love with its joy clears and sharpens the vision.

Helen Keller

Love knows no mean or measure.

Phineas Fletcher

There is nothing nobler or more admirable than when two people who see eye-to-eye keep house as man and wife, confounding their enemies and delighting their friends.

Homer

Knowing is the most profound kind of love, giving someone the gift of knowledge about yourself.

Marsha Norman

The giving of love is an education in itself.

Eleanor Roosevelt

Joy is a net of love by which you can catch souls.

Mother Teresa

When two people love each other, they don't look at each other, they look in the same direction.

———

Ginger Rogers

The best and most beautiful
things in the world cannot be
seen or even touched. They
must be felt with the heart.

Helen Keller

Life is a flower of which
love is the honey.

Victor Hugo

If you would be loved, love
and be lovable.

Benjamin Franklin

To love someone means to
see him as God intended him.

Fyodor Dostoevski

Love is a power too strong
to be overcome by anything
but flight.

———————

Miguel de Cervantes

There is no heaven like
mutual love.

———

George Granville

First we make up, and then
we fight:
(A miserable wretch am I!)
To live with her's beyond me
quite,
And yet without her I should
die.

———

Jean Desmarets

No one perfectly loves God
who does not perfectly love
some of his creatures.

———————

Marguerite de Valois

No one knows how it is
that with one glance a boy
can break through into a girl's
heart.

Nancy Thayer

Many waters cannot quench love, nor can the floods drown it.

Song of Solomon 8:7
(NKJV)

One of the oldest human
needs is having someone to
wonder where you are when
you don't come home at
night.

————

Margaret Mead

Age does not protect you from love. But love, to some extent, protects you from age.

Jeanne Moreau

The heart that loves is always young.

Greek proverb

In a successful marriage, there is no such thing as one's way. There is only the way of both, only the bumpy, dusty, difficult, but always mutual path.

Phyllis McGinley

When you love someone
all your saved up wishes start
coming out.

Elizabeth Bowen

Love keeps the cold out
better than a cloak.

Henry Wadsworth
Longfellow

An archaeologist is the best husband any woman can have: The older she gets, the more interested he is in her.

Agatha Christie

Love comforteth like
sunshine after rain.

William Shakespeare

W e cannot really love
anybody with whom we never
laugh.

Agnes Repplier

Love is space and time
measured by the heart.

Marcel Proust

Love is wont rather to
ascend than descend.

———

Thomas Fuller

Love is, above all, the gift of oneself.

Jean Anouilh

W e don't love qualities, we love persons; sometimes by reason of their defects as well as of their qualities.

———————

Jacques Maritain

There is no fear in love; but perfect love casts out fear.

1 John 4:18 (NKJV)

Those marriages generally abound most with love and constancy that are preceded by a long courtship. The passion should strike root and gather strength before marriage be grafted on it.

Joseph Addison

For lovers, touch is metamorphosis. All the parts of their bodies seem to change, and they become something different and better.

John Cheever

There is more pleasure in
loving than in being beloved.

———

Thomas Fuller

Love is the irresistible desire
to be desired irresistibly.

Louis Ginsberg

Love is that condition in which the happiness of another person is essential to your own.

Robert A. Heinlein

The pleasure of love is in loving, and we are made happier by the passion we experience than by that which we inspire.

Francois, Duc de La Rochefoucauld

He who finds a wife finds a good thing, and obtains favor from the Lord.

Proverbs 18:22 (NKJV)

How many loved your
  moments of glad grace,
And loved your beauty with
  love false or true:
But one man loved the
  pilgrim soul in you,
And loved the sorrows of your
  changing face.

———

William Butler Yeats

To the One
I love

There is no harvest for the
heart alone;
The seed of love must be
Eternally
Resown.

Anne Morrow
Lindbergh

To love is the great amulet
that makes this world a
garden.

Robert Louis
Stevenson

Love is the master key that opens the gates of happiness.

Oliver Wendell
Holmes

In literature as in love, we are astonished at what is chosen by others.

Andre Maurois

I believe that love cannot be bought except with love, and he who has a good wife wears heaven in his hat.

John Steinbeck

A man is not where he lives, but where he loves.

Latin Proverb

It is love, not reason, that is stronger than death.

———————

Thomas Mann

One loving heart sets
another on fire.

———

St. Augustine

It is difficult to know at what moment love begins; it is less difficult to know that it has begun.

Henry Wadsworth Longfellow

W ho travels for love finds
a thousand miles not longer
than one.

—————

Japanese proverb

Love seems the swiftest, but it is the slowest of all growths. No man or woman really knows what perfect love is until they have been married a quarter of a century.

———

Mark Twain

No, there's nothing half so
sweet in life
As love's young dream.

Thomas Moore

One cannot be strong without love. For love is not an irrelevant emotion; it is the blood of life, the power of reunion of the separated.

Paul Tillich

Love is an act of endless
forgiveness, a tender look
which becomes a habit.

——————

Peter Ustinov

Falling in love is easy;
growing in love must be
worked at with determination
as well as imagination.

———

Lesley Barfoot

Only little boys and old men sneer at love.

Louis Auchincloss

This is one of the miracles of love: it gives . . . a power of seeing through its own enchantments and yet not being disenchanted.

———

C. S. Lewis

I hold it true, whate'er
   befall;
   I feel it when I sorrow
      most;
'Tis better to have loved and
   lost
Than never to have loved at
   all.

Alfred, Lord Tennyson

Take this with warmest love,
Tho' fans are, as a rule,
Considered efficacious
In keeping people cool.

Love begins when a person feels another person's needs to be as important as his own.

Harry S. Sullivan

I have lived long enough to know, that the evening glow of love has its own riches and splendor.

Benjamin Disraeli

Love is a great thing, a great good in every wise; it alone maketh light every heavy thing and beareth evenly every uneven thing.

Thomas à Kempis

To love deeply in one direction makes us more loving in all others.

Madame Swetchnie

Love one another; as I have loved you, that you also love one another.

John 13:34 (NKJV)

It is a truth universally acknowledged that a single man in possession of a good fortune must be in want of a wife.

Jane Austen

The essential dimension to a marriage is the quality of peace.

Robin Scroggs

In marriage you never arrive,
you are always on the road.

Patricia Gundry

Love is the salt that savors
the whole of life and drives
away the mists so that the sun
may eternally shine.

George Matthew
Adams

To marry a woman or man for beauty is like buying a house for its coat of paint.

___

American Proverb

Love is giving freely,
expecting nothing in return.
Law concerns itself with an
equitable exchange, this for
that. Law is made necessary
by people; love is made
possible by God.

———————

Mary Carson

Marriages are made in heaven, but they are lived on earth.

George P. Weiss

No cord or cable can draw
so forcibly, or bind so fast, as
love can do with a single
thread.

———————

Robert Burton

To be a woman is to have the same needs and longings as a man. We need love and we wish to give it.

Liv Ullman

The love we give away is
the only love we keep.

Elbert Hubbard

Love doesn't just sit there, like a stone, it has to be made, like bread; remade all the time, made new.

Ursula K. LeGuin

Marriage is three parts love and seven parts forgiveness of sins.

Langdon Mitchell

There is a comfort in the
strength of love;
'Twill make a thing endurable,
which else
Would overset the brain, or
break the heart.

William Wordsworth

Respect is what we owe;
love, what we give.

———

Philip James Bailey

You can give without loving, but you cannot love without giving.

Amy Carmichael

A happy man marries the girl he loves, but a happier man loves the girl he marries.

Anonymous

It is impossible to love and be wise.

————

Francis Bacon

Most of us love from our need to love, not because we find someone deserving.

Nikki Giovanni

Two souls with but a single thought,
Two hearts that beat as one.

Maria Lovell

A loving heart is the truest wisdom.

Charles Dickens

To love anyone is nothing
other than to wish that
person good.

St. Thomas Aquinas

The man who is in love for the first time, even if his love is unrequited, is a godlike being.

Heinrich Heine

Love, all alike, no season
knows, nor clime,
Nor hours, days, months,
which are the rags of time.

———

John Donne

Love is swift, sincere, pious, pleasant, generous, strong, patient, faithful, prudent, long-suffering, manly, and never seeking her own; for wheresoever a man seeketh his own, there he falleth from love.

Thomas à Kempis

Love is the feeling that makes a woman make a man make a fool of himself.

———

Anonymous

Love is the basic need of human nature, for without it life is disrupted emotionally, mentally, spiritually and physically.

———————

Karl Menninger

Love looks not with the
eyes, but with the mind;
And therefore is winged
Cupid painted blind.

William Shakespeare

Where there is room in the heart, there is always room in the house.

Thomas Moore

As soon as you cannot keep anything from a woman, you love her.

Paul Geraldy

Where love is concerned,
too much is not even enough.

Pierre-Augustin de
Beaumarchais

To keep the fire burning
brightly, there's one easy rule:
keep the two logs together,
near enough to keep each
other warm and far enough
apart—about a finger's
breath—for breathing room.
Good fire, good marriage,
same rule.

———

Marnie Reed Crowell

The supreme happiness of life is the conviction of being loved for yourself, or, more correctly, being loved in spite of yourself.

Victor Hugo

Love is all we have, the
only way that each can help
the other.

Euripides

There is no way under the sun of making a man worthy of love, except by loving him.

Thomas Merton

Love is not love until love's vulnerable.

Theodore Roethke

Love is all we have, the
only way that each can help
the other.

Euripides

Love is a light that casts a
shadow on the sun.

Donald Danford

A man is only as good as what he loves.

Saul Bellow

P eople who are sensible
about love are incapable of it.

———

Douglas Yates

To love someone is to be
the only one to see a miracle
invisible to others.

———

Francois Mauriac

They dream in courtship,
but in wedlock wake.

Alexander Pope

Love suffers long and is kind; love does not envy; love does not parade itself, is not puffed up; does not behave rudely, does not seek its own, is not provoked, thinks no evil; . . . bears all things, believes all things, hopes all things, endures all things. Love never fails.

1 Corinthians 13:4–8 (NKJV)

A man is already halfway
in love with any woman who
listens to him.

Brendan Francis

The heart has reasons
which the reason cannot
understand.

——————

Blaise Pascal